T0208702

JUVENILE AND NONSENSICAL

Written by

Michael Richardson Jr.

Illustrated by Bryan Golden

authorHOUSE®

AuthorHouse™
1663 Liberty Drive
Bloomington, IN 47403
www.authorhouse.com
Phone: 1-800-839-8640

First published by AuthorHouse   3/2/2011

ISBN: 978-1-4567-3479-4 (sc)
ISBN: 978-1-4567-3478-7 (e)

Library of Congress Control Number: 2011901713

Printed in the United States of America

Any people depicted in stock imagery provided by Thinkstock are models, and such images are being used for illustrative purposes only. Certain stock imagery © Thinkstock.

This book is printed on acid-free paper.

"Never Give Up. Never Surrender."

Captain Jason Nesmith
Dean Parisot's Galaxy Quest

SPECIAL THANKS

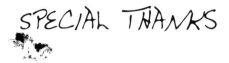

I would like to thank the following friends and family for their support and dedication to the project. Without them this may have never existed.

I would like to thank my parents Michael and Byllie for their encouragement and understanding.

I would like to thank Bryan Golden for giving this project new life with his extraordinary artwork.

Thank you Domminick Forrest for your poetic contribution of "Lone" to this project

Thank you Bryant Gerome Morris Jr. and Jonathan Smith for all your support

Thank you Amanda Tovar for your artistic inspiration.

Thank you Richard Heffelfinger for your help creating the cover. He can be contacted through Slackslash.com

Lastly, I would like to thank the writing center of California State University of San Bernardino. Thank you for enduring my many visits and helping me shape this book into what it is today.

CONTENTS

my SEXY EPIPHANY

The red sun is setting

And my greatest hour approaches

As I stare at a metaphor

Blood red sky

Before entering the grave

To meet the siren of my nightmares.

There she lay

Encased in stone

Silently drawing me near

With her siren song

Crafted specifically for my ears.

Do I release her?

Do I destroy her ?

Or do I destroy us all?

This quandary rest on my shoulders alone.

I can't resist

My lust got the better of me

I open Pandora's Box

With a heart-filled smile.

I gaze upon her true beauty

The dark crimson on her lips

The golden wheat colored hair

The ghastly white of her skin

Now radiating from the light

Of a jealous moon overhead.

Her hands rest neatly folded on her bosom

Her corset kindly exposes

Just enough to spark my imagination

As I place a red rose in her hands.

Hark, she hath awaken

Releasing a bone chilling scream

Allowing me to witness upon her fangs.

She stares wildly

In fear of my elaborate wooden dagger

That I raised over her heart

Then ensnares my eye

And promises me the world.

I return the gaze

And a tear leaves my eye

Rushing off my face

As I strike

Mercy and vengeance expressed as one.

Forgive me my love

Auf Wiendersehen

We will always have my nightmares.

I AM THE NIGHT

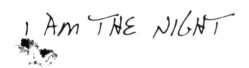

I awake to the symphony of the night
Its melodic trance induces much delight
Driving me towards less conventional affairs
I obey it blindly without much care
I bask in its moonlight without vexation
For its silver light brings rejuvenation
And power to walk its streets
While others lie fast asleep
Allowing me to embrace the darkness in solitude
While the orchestra plays keeping me subdued

FIERY DISPLEASURES

Troubled eyes gaze upon the pale moon light
Contemplating her heinous plan for tonight
Knowing her life would never be the same
Once she resurrects the devious and untamed
Angel of darkness that fell far from grace
Sentenced to remain in an inhospitable place
For the rest of eternity, the end of all time
Until he found his way to Francesca's mind
Promising pleasures of unspeakable power
Preparing her for this day and this very hour.

With one final look she pulls a veil over her eyes
Preparing to commence the ritual before sunrise
She walks in a room lit only by candle light
That illuminated a terrifying demonic shrine
Where she places a dog's head to make it complete
Then smears its blood encompassing her feet
Taking a scalpel and cutting her finger
Holding it in place watching the blood drops linger
Dripping to form the shape of the damned
Connecting the dots to complete a pentagram
Whilst she chanted words the devil put in her head
From the hidden Catholic Book of the Dead
The evil words cause the dog's eyes to glow

Indicating that something was stirring below

A mysterious wind leaves her in shadow

Until large flames appeared and billowed

And a mysterious being stands in the wild flames

Saying "At last this world is mine to reclaim."

As the fire died down she got her first vision

Of the handsome angel the gospels envisioned

On his person he held not a weapon

And to Francesca looked an innocent shunned from Heaven

She fell for this beast without any intellection

Forgetting that he was God's greatest abomination

 She runs to him with loving arms

Hoping he will forever keep her from harm

And as she stands silently in his powerful embrace

He caresses her with one arm around her waist

Saying, "Francesca you will forever be mine,

But first you must leave this mortal body behind."

She paused for a moment not believing her ears

She asked, "What exactly do you mean my dear?"

He whispered in her ear causing her to lose control

As he spoke directly to her very soul

Commanding her to take her own life

And Francesca obediently walked towards the surgical knife

With the blade in her grasp she could not withstand

The blade plunged through her flesh and she died by her own hands

As Satan watched on with his face all a grin

In approval of Francesca's ultimate sin

And he summoned her soul to stand by his side

To watch the world as it withers and dies

And everything that she held dear from the past
Was reduced to smoldering pieces of ash
Now she wanders the globe, heart full of regret
Feeling her reward for her treason was much worse than death

FEEL MY NUMBNESS

Emotion flutters like butterflies around me
Blowing in the wind through blackened trees
Moving too fast and evading my grasp
As I reach for them the emotions don't last
They burst like bubbles upon my touch
Their residue on my metallic heart begins to rust
Rendering me useless and on my knees
As I watch the emotions flutter away from me.

GIFT FROM THE HEAVENS

A loud alarm disturbs your slumber
Still half asleep and can barely read the numbers
On the clock's display that sits on the night stand
So you wipe out the sleep with the back of your hand
And brush aside the curtain to look out the window
Then stare curiously above and below
Seeing nothing but neighbors looking baffled
Head out the house to find out why everyone's rattled
You step out the door and into the light
And can't help but wonder why everything is so bright
You turn and look up not a moment too soon
Gazing up in the sky at a falling full moon

Now the people are quickly stirring
Adrenaline is causing motion blurring
As you watch the moon fall from the sky
The first thing you think is, why?
Watching people in a panic
Acting crazy and acting manic
Seconds, minutes, hours, irrelevant time
Inevitability is soon to arrive
Is this the work of God or Lucifer?
They're your final moments; whatever you prefer
The abundant fear causing a mental wall

Shielding you from your wife and children's calls
Their voices you can't bear to hear
Now that you know that their deaths are near
Life's a bitch, this much is true
But you have to admit you have a beautiful view.

THAT'S THE WAY OF THE WORLD

A child lies uncomfortably bound on the floor
While an armed stranger stands before a door
Smiling while yelling is heard from the next room
The child closes his eyes hoping it will all be over soon
But jumped when he heard two loud sounds
Only silence until someone came out leaving two bodies on the ground
The child could not believe his eyes
And could not help but feel that he was going to die
Then another masked man walked in his direction
Leaned down beside him and said, "I have a confession.
I did not want to do what I did tonight,
But I had to support my children and my wife.
Some things in life are beyond your control
This may be hard to understand since your only six years old
When people are desperate they'll do terrible things
Like murdering your parents for expensive wedding rings.
Unfortunately this is a lesson that you won't learn.
I can't afford to let you live so it's now your turn.

...To be continued

15

ON THEIR PATHS TO RIGHTEOUSNESS

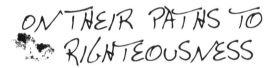

Flying gracefully into the light
To escape a world of darkness
Shedding a lifetime of tears
As it searches for a brighter tomorrow
Coincidentally darkening every inch
Depressing every living thing
Dampening the spirits of all
The Mourning Dove

WHAT WOULD YOU DO?

Bullets fly in every direction

And you have not a vest for protection

You pray to God for a pass of omission

And remember you're right next to the entrance

A passage to safety and also your freedom

Their fates are all sealed so who cares if you leave them?

You're not a God or one of omnipotence

You'll atone for your sins by some act of penance

As you reach for the door you hear cries of help

As you look through the window you think to yourself

Is it better to live as a coward or die a savior?

Makes you ponder human behavior

CRIMSON TEARS

Do you know the one who sheds crimson tears?

Many believe that they are for someone dear

Others suspect some kind of deception

I suppose it could be a kind of rendition

Of pain and suffering that one endures for a while

But that won't explain that awkward smile

With blood-soaked teeth that are all a grin

An insidious smile holding secretive sins

Despite our curiosity we are far too shy

We can only suspect that there's more to the tears than meets the eye.

EASIER FOR SOME THAN OTHERS

A great pressure builds on a trigger

A fifty-fifty chance; go figure

To violate your pocket in hopes of profit

Or perhaps there's more to this awkward portrait

He's taken your wallet and got what he was after

So why does this peculiar man still loiter

He pulls back the hammer with no hesitation

You now find yourself in the worst situation

You beg him for mercy as you tremble with fright

He answers while smiling and says, "No not tonight."

THE TRAGIC PRINCE

A black knight rides out of the fire
And yet this conditioned warrior does not perspire
He rides with such passion, such dedication
He has not time for ill-fated contemplation
The fate of two kingdoms is placed in his hands
Can't crack under pressure of such extreme demands
As he gallops towards a large stone fortress
He comes face to face with an evil sorceress
Who uses magic and trickery to stop his ascend
Up many flights of stairs to free his childhood friend
So with his shield in one hand and sword in the other
He fights his way up to rescue his lover
Once he reached the top he kicked down the door
And saw his wife to be, whom he loved and adored
But before they could celebrate they heard the cry of a dragon
A size neither the princess nor knight could fathom
With haste she ran towards the knight for protection
Unfortunately it was already too late to avoid detection
Without hesitation they tried to escape the tower
Knowing all too well of the dragon's endless power
But before they were half way down the dragon lifted its tail
And with one mighty blow caused their escape to fail.

Large stones fall down as the tower gives way

Both knight and princess fall promptly to their graves

The dust had settled and for a while nothing had moved

Which hinted that both the princess and knight were doomed

Then out of nowhere did two hands emerge

One holding a battered shield, the other a sword

With the strength that he mustered he pulled his way out

And his concern for the princess caused him to shout

Almost immediately he dug through the rubble

He could not help but feel that the princess was in trouble

It took several moments, but the princess was found

But not to his liking she was still and made not a sound

Despite his emotions the knight did not cry

Even though the death of his lover made him feel empty inside

While the knight was distracted the dragon did flee

But the knight did give chase with his mighty steed

The direction it flew was straight towards his hometown

He knew that the dragon would burn the town down

Despite his best efforts the dragon was too quick

And the sight on arrival made him feel awfully sick

Every man, woman, and child were all dead

Including his father; now a skeleton with a crown on his head

With great anger the knight put his fist to the sand

For his family's kingdom was now useless land

He swore he'd hunt the dragon until the end of time

And make him pay for such an awful crime

The crown he did take; a representation of his history

Then wore it atop his head to boast his ancestry

He quickly rode out to get his revenge

And searched the whole continent for the dragon's din

Until one day he caught a glimpse of it in flight

Then followed it to its cave and made plans to attack at night

As the sinking sun set and the orange sky turned black

The knight prepared himself for the attack

Next he silently infiltrated the lair of the beast

Walking cautiously so as not to become the dragon's feast

As he got nearer he could feel and hear the dragon's breath

A wrong move at this point would be bad for his health

Since the cave was so dark it obstructed his vision

Not being able to see his foe made it hard to make a decision

At that moment the knight thought about luring the dragon outside

But was surprised when he saw two blood-thirsty red eyes

It was at this moment that he began to feel some regret

He had a feeling this was going to be a fight that he would never forget

His sword he did swing while the dragon was off guard

For he knew that once alerted defeating it would be quite hard

The elaborate sword struck the dragon across the eye

It was quite apparent that the knight was not afraid to die

The dragon wined and cried out in pain

Breathing out enough fire to light up the cave

Fire hit the ceiling and spread all over the vicinity

And fluttered to the ground covering the knights body

The smoldering ashes did cool grey upon the black steel

So the burning sensation on his flesh he did not feel

The dragon's head sprung forth with mouth open wide

Caused the knight to dodge knowing there was nowhere to hide

The knight had to keep moving no matter how sore

But he had to get close enough to use his sword

Every time he got close a fireball did blast

From the dragon's mouth making it hard to get past

And at that moment he decided to change his strategy

Or he feared this event would surely end in tragedy

He back stepped to the entrance where he heard stormy weather

As he kept his eye on the dragon from behind his only shelter

His battered shield was now heavily charred

But the knight did not worry for he knew it was not far

Rumbling closely behind was the dragon looking quite vicious

But why his opponent was leaving made it feel rather suspicious

Once they were outside the knight looked up to the heavens

As rainfall fell, running down his armor and weapons

The intensity of the rainfall grew stronger causing puddle reflective

Where the dragon could be seen fighting much less effective

The rainy weather gave the knight a decent advantage

And knew that with it he could do much more damage

He ran through the fire that went a shorter distance

The fire the dragon breathed now provided little resistance

His glimmering sword cut through the fire into the beasts arm

However he was unsure if he was causing it much harm.

To his surprise the dragon countered with its razor sharp claw

Brushing him aside making him tumble like a rag doll

Making him lose his crown and shattering his armor

Revealing his bare flesh that showed off his muscular figure

The handsome knight stood up and brushed back his hair

Then gave his opponent a menacing stare

He only picked up his sword and got back into the fight

Moving with great agility because he was now light

While he was running the dragon swung with his right arm

But the knight had jumped over it without much alarm

He managed to grab hold during the dragon's last attack

And with great determination climbed up the dragon's back

The dragon did his best to shake off the knight

But the knight would not budge as he held on tight

He just kept climbing the dragon's scaly coat

Until he reached a vital spot and put his sword in its throat

The large wound spurt out fire and blood

And the dragon lost consciousness and fell down in the mud

Our victorious knight jumped down from the dragon to pray to the gods

For a rainstorm in the middle of summer is quite odd

He jumped on his steed and set out for the kingdom of Santa Cruz

To speak to his deceased lover's father and give him the bad news

But when he arrived the king sentenced him for treason

The knight angrily questioned him, "For what reason?"

"For secretly plotting to take over my throne."

"Please listen to reason king. I had my own throne at home."

Unfortunately his logical explanation the king did disregard

And without hesitation summoned the royal guards

Very angrily he hacked and slashed through them all

Leaving them in horrific positions; one was even pinned to the wall

The king tried to escape through an old secret passage

That led all the way out to the edge of the village

 But the knight could not be so easily fooled

For he and the princess played in those halls since they were both two

He had to find out who was behind this elaborate operation

For the king would pursue him until his execution

It was not long before the king was in sight

And when the king saw the knight it gave him a fright

The king was chased to the top of the mountain

Until there was nowhere to run his eyes watered like a fountain

"My boy," the king said, "I have done you a great inequity.

I am the culprit behind this whole tragedy.

This was all a grand scheme to steal your family's land.

The sorceress, dragon, and princess were all in on the plan.

Can you find it in your heart to grant me some mercy?"

Impetuously the knight responded, "Sorry, but my blade is still thirsty."

All throughout the land a bloody scream could be heard

And when the knight returned to the kingdom no one said a word.

The knight slouched in the throne while wearing a frown

Even as the servants approached to give him the crown.

So my friends, this is the story that minstrels do sings

About how the tragic prince had become a king.

EARLY SENTENCE

A child is a wonderful gift

That gives parents a reason to live

A day to be marked in celebration

The product of self-gratification

You've fallen to a slippery slope

Knowing your only gift for them is hope

You hope that your child will grow to be strong

And live a fruitful life that's long

Although in life there are no guarantees

They could face countless atrocities

Sickness, old age, death, or worse

Thoughts that never occur during intercourse

No time for regret or for repentance

Just know every birth carries a child's sentence

JESUS WALKS

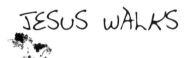

Our beloved Jesus walks the Earth

And steps amongst our ashes and dirt

Walking forward with mild eyes bright

As scorching fires brighten the night

He calls to us as loud as he can

But hears no cry from child, woman, nor man.

Despite his calls there's no one running

For we brought about Armageddon before his second coming

FATHER OF THY FATHER

Allow me to break from typical ideology
And only take this poem as curious philosophy
But what if the creator had not yet been created
Just another concept waiting to be invented
For the advancements in science and biology
To be used to make God a reality
A being of unthinkable perfection
Would we be worthy of his affection
Or bring about unspeakable destruction
The concept alone brings forth so many questions
Would he be the God believers envision
A strong ruler of strength and precision
Or a tyrant ruling with fear and rage
Condemning us all to start a new page
The next evolution for all of mankind
A new sentient being completely refined
Would they accept him or revert into heathens
Or is that the true nature of being human?

KRASH

Twilight approaches and sky turns blue
Why can I not forget about you?
Let out a sigh and engage my turn signal
My lust for you has got to be fatal.
As I merge to the left I pick up the phone
And dial her number to reach her at home
I had a feeling that she would not pick up
But today it appears I am not out of luck
I give her a greeting but she did not reply
My heart skipped a beat; I thought that I died
She questioned my call and told me it's over
Quickly I told her that I was completely sober
Begging her to give me another chance
Ensuring her I can be a better man
She hung up the phone without saying a word
Only the dial tone on the phone could be heard
I dropped the phone and agreed it was for the best
Then let go of the wheel and drew a cross on my chest
Closed my eyes and let the car drive up the street
Set the cruise control and destination to eternal sleep.

LUV A LIE

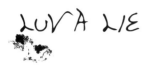

I told my love I loved her dearly

It was a lie, she saw it clearly

And responded to me the same

That she could think no other name

Except mine, which was not true

Her beautiful exterior is see through

It shows her heart as black as coal

Which reminds me of my own soul

This fact alone keeps us near

And is the only reason this love adheres

WHAT I HAVE ALWAYS WANTED TO SAY

Why do I freeze when you walk by?

Or find it hard to stare into your eyes?

Why do I shake when you are near?

Or melt when your lovely voice enters my ear?

Why do I grow silent when I have much to say ?

How often have I put it off for another day ?

Am I going about this all wrong ?

Should I have just said, "I love you" all along?

BOY MAGNETIZE GIRL

Boy and girl

Both destined to meet

Pulled into the air

Off of their feet

With incredible force

Through busy streets

Over each tall edifice

Into busy crowds

Even through an office

Causing much destruction

As they make their journey

Through numerous obstructions

Until finally they unite

In each other's arms

Holding on tight

Like a magnetic reaction

Their physics lesson

The law of attraction

THE PROMISE

As I stare into her eyes
I begin to feel as if I died
Drowned in the black pools of space
Yet I crave no other place
A beam of hope she does bestow
Lost in her iris, the great unknown
I pray thee save me from my sorrow
And I will promise that before tomorrow
You'll have my soul and heart entire
For forever even after my life force expires

90 SECOND HINDSIGHT

Falling glass floats back shimmering with light
As the bullet flies back to the gun with an eye over the sight
The bullet entering and exiting repairing torn pieces of brain
As an unsuspecting husband straightens a face winced with pain
He takes a toothbrush out his mouth wiping the smile from his face
While a deeply troubled woman slowly drops the gun to her waist
And the tears on her face rolled back like a reversed faucet
Her cries eerily sound backwards as she walks backwards to the closet
Where she put the .45 back in its designated box
Then back steps to the phone on the side of the bed and talks
Saying "Go gotta I ," before her friend starts talking
Giving her the news that her husband has been cheating

TO FELLOW LOSERS

It seems we share some common ground
Let me show you what I have found
Your life has fallen into fate's hands
Destroying your hopes, dreams, and plans
You look for aid from the gods above
Only to find no mercy, remorse, or love
You can cry, complain, or curse his name
Release your anger to keep yourself sane
Whatever your choice your fate is set
You can try to play the hand your dealt
You're going to lose regardless the choice
Your say in life has been out-voiced
But do not worry and do not fear
The next point may bring some cheer
When all is said and all is done
Fate will come for everyone
Wealth and love the dead can't use
So in the end we all lose.

A GIRL NAMED NOSTALGIA

For years she sat at the window pane
Her only doorway to the outside world
Whether it's bright or dark with rain
A most humble and forgiving girl
Watching the world pass her by
Losing herself to the passing time
Receiving neither a wave nor "hi"
A punishment without committing a crime
To watch the men for whom she holds lust
Take the hands of those less deserving
Shattering her dreams to a fine dust
She should let go, no need for preserving
And when they kiss, a terrible anguish
All actions to cause her internal strife
No one sees her reaching out or languish
Until one day she ended her life
By cutting her wrist while taking a shower
Watching her life rinse down the drain
Even today her grave has not a single flower
And dust builds on her window pane

I DREAM ALIVE

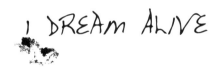

From the moment I wake
To the time I close my eyes
Do I ponder my mistake
Losing myself in all my lies
Seeking reality
In the world I created
From numerous actualities
Are they interrelated?
I can't really recall
Memories from long ago
Oh do I bawl
If only I could let go
Of these delusional desires
And find the world so true
If I was not such a liar
I could find my way back to you

MISERABLE TEENS

Thousands of books hold you down
A sea of debt can make you drown
Dividing the weak from the strong
Was the educational model all along
Looked at with such high expectation
Throw responsibility into the equation
Can lead to drugs and alcoholism
An adolescent's form of masochism
Pain warms the blood when the world is cold
Keeps them alive until they're old enough to console

PRIORITIES

Another day another dollar
Creates obstacles for young scholars
Illusions of wealth exchanged for hours
Make them forget about their flower
Of knowledge that gives them wings
Only concern them with material things
Finally when they're old and gray
And all their hours have been spent away
Will they realize that knowledge is free
And perhaps invest in better philosophy

STUCK

Stuck is a place where nothing goes right
Where goals and destinations are kept from sight
Stuck is a feeling you feel in your gut
Notice the chips are down, You're down on your luck
Nothing is coming and nothing is going
Everything's there since no progress is showing
You measure the good and compare to the bad
A lack of activity leaves no conclusion to be had
So is there a remedy for such a dilemma?
If you find one be sure to post the data

LONE

By Domminick Forrest

A lonely loner sitting silently screaming

Searching for something already found: a meaning

Increasing the distance and stranded by choice

Things come from his mouth that are deeper than his voice

Looking to the heavens but finding no guidance

Resisting assistance in youthful defiance

Lost in a forest of questioning thoughts

Fighting a battle that need not be fought

Waving his hand bye, too far to ask why

Too proud to cry, and too young to die

Turning from those whom he once called his friends

Unbeknownst to him it's his pride he defends

Lone dreamer watching from the window of his mind

Walking a new path unsure of what he'll find

A lonely loner sitting silently screaming

Searching for something already found: a meaning

CANVAS OF REGRET

Deep in a house in a downstairs room
A picture develops in the womb
The mind of a woman lost in lament
Wondering where her innocence went
Brush and canvas meet making truth
Trying with difficulty to reclaim her youth
But with white and vibrant red
She exposes her inner desires instead
Painting with vigor and with precision
Leaving the canvas with an alarming vision
A ghostly white body encompassed by dark
An explosion of red depicts a broken heart
She makes death obvious and plain to see
As bloody butterflies flutter where her head use to be

my CLEMENTIA

Please, my beauty, grant me mercy
Before my courage duth desert me
Alas, even your tears, a heavenly rain
Will not be able to cure me of my pain
With innocent hands so soft and gentle
Place a bullet right through my temple
Free me from this prison, this hollow shell
Only death can free me from this hell
For I have lost my way, my soul, my purpose
Letting my anger, regret, and depression surface
For years I have worn this Janus mask
Which is why I have given you this task
My love, my life, my only friend
My life is yours and yours alone to end

CONFUSING TIMES

How is a young man supposed to feel?

A grandson to a generation of hate

A son to a generation of progress

A man in a generation of confusion

How's a young man suppose to lead?

A grandson to a generation of heroes

A son to a generation of legends

A Man in a generation of forgotten memory

How's a young man suppose to continue?

A grandson to a generation that fought the impossible

A son to a generation that survived the impossible

A man in a generation that made the impossible possible.

WHEN IS BAD NOT GOOD ENOUGH?

Stocks and planes have fallen amidst,
The citizens who are struggling.
Where's the stories of long time bliss,
Amidst political finger pointing?
Are the stories of better times,
Simply forgotten or nonexistent?
Maybe there is a better rhyme,
To explain this special instance.
Could the answer just be overlooked,
To keep our minds at ease?
Or network's idea of good news
Won't keep the investors pleased?

my BROTHERHOOD ENDED A FRIENDSHIP

My brother and I were very close,
Yet now we are far apart.
We used to talk of everything,
Yet now our talks grow silent.
I guess it was our closeness

Our once large house that held us both,
Not big enough for the both of us.
Where closest of kin once stayed,
They now stay shunned.
I guess it was our closeness

I always wondered why it came,
Our periods of grief.
Today I am wiser and have an answer,
The conclusion was very simple.
I simply let my brother get too close

WAR

What is War?

The greatest poem unwritten

The greatest song unsung

The tallest building unbuilt

The hardest problem unsolved

The greatest scientific discovery lost

the deadliest disease uncured

The greatest leaders of tomorrow unborn

The most important lessons forgotten

That's all war is.

A TALE OF TWO KILLERS

It was the middle of nowhere with a desert theme
So far from civilization no one could hear you scream
But regardless the setting and regardless the heat
Two young gunslingers were destined to meet.
One wore a bowler derby hat and a black bandana
A memoir he carried from his home in Montana
He was known as Tex by his closest of kin
The "End of the Line" to those who weren't his friend.
The other young gunslinger's name was Clint
Well, we'll just say that he was bloodthirsty gent
Ironically his apparel was that of a coroner
An interesting look for a gun slinging warrior.
With his top hat he resembled the 16th president
But his clean shaven face made him look more prevalent.
They stared at each other with much concentration
Wondering what the other would do in this odd situation
As they continued to stare in each other's eyes
The wind picked up blowing dust and a cliché tumbled by
Then instantaneously Clint made his move
For Clint was a man that had something to prove
He pulled out his Winchester from under his coat
And aimed it so delicately for his opponents throat
Tex quickly jumped out of the bullet's path
Returned fire showing his double barrel shotgun's wrath

The fired shells expand into hundreds of pellets

But Clint just stood still and rolled up a cigarette

As the pellets headed straight towards his body

He quickly drew his pistols and shot each pellet individually

Tex holstered his shotgun and pulled out his knife

As this was going to be a different kind of fight

Clint followed suit with a Katana and Wakizashi

Which he surprisingly wielded like a Miyamoto Musashi

They came together separated only by ten paces

So close they could see the sweat run down each other's faces

Clint jumped out towards Tex and caught a fist to his chin

And despite the pain managed to maintain a grin

He swung his sword which was caught by Tex's teeth

A feat that proved Tex was a man of a different breed

With great frustration Clint reached for his spare blade

While Tex Desperately looked for some kind of aid

Alas for Tex no luck could be found

But as the blade drew near his keen ears heard a sound

That brought a confident look back to his face

And Clint stopped when the ground began to shake

The ground was trembling and the pebbles did rattle

From the hooves of the quickly approaching cattle

"Stampede," Tex exclaimed before the two spread

"Dammit," Clint yelled and his face went beet red

Both men did their best to get out the way
After all neither of them wanted to die that day
In a matter of moments the herd came and went
Tex could only suspect that they were God sent
So he drew a cross on his chest and looked to the sky
Thanking God for saving his miserable hide
But as he kissed the cross that hung from his throat
He saw Clint get up and dust off his coat
As he looked at Tex he reached into his pocket
Pulled out his watch, gasped, and took off like a rocket
"I'll get you next time our paths cross again
But for right now this fight must end
Although I would love to stay and take your life
Now that I am late I face a tougher battle.. with my wife"
Tex cringed and wished him luck on his trip
Sighed and said, "That poor fella's whipped"
Tex straightened his hat and fixed his bandana
And continued on his journey to his home in Montana.

THAT'S THE WAY OF THE WORLD PT 2

An icy muzzle rests on the temple

of a frightened boy who shakes and trembles

Trying his hardest to stay strong

For his parents that are now gone

As two heartless men watch from above

Both with guns in their leather gloves

Who smile as the young boy cries

But freeze when they hear a noise in the skies

A bright light pours in through the window

From a helicopter shining its light on the house below

Police cars are quick to follow suit

Officers step out of their cars ready to shoot

One screamed, "Come out. We know you're in there."

Which gave the robbers a significant scare

In a panic his masked partner opened fire

Creating a situation extremely dire

The masked man stopped shooting, but a shot did blast

A bullet shot through the glass, then his partner's mask

Angrily he watched as his friend fell to the floor

And with the boy in hand walked out the front door

Cautiously, he aimed his gun at boy's head

Screaming, "One wrong move and he's dead."

The police officers put their guns down

70

Which means it's all up to the snipers now
Who watch as the boy and masked man head towards a car
The officers smile, knowing that he won't get too far
The gun drops from the child who is now safe from harm
The snipers quickly take aim at the robber's arms
They get the approval and the shot is made
The bullet connects and they save the day
A downed robber starts to huff and puff
While the police tackle him and apply hand cuffs
Quickly the traumatized boy is taken to safety
And is surrounded by people concerned with his frailty
The robber is promptly placed in a squad car's back seat
Then glares at the boy as they drive up the street
A sniper comes to sit next to the boy
He shakes his hand saying, "My name is Roy.
I know this night has forever changed your life
I'm sorry you lost both of you parents tonight
But the world is full of strange human beings
That do terrible things with mysterious meaning
Some things in life are beyond your control
This might be hard to understand since your only six years old
But you will find as you grow old
That the world can be harsh and cold
However, the world can also be a beautiful place
Full of people who exemplify God's grace
So let go of your anger and let go of your hate
Or you too might suffer the robber's fate."

THE BLACK LOTUS

Long long ago in rural Japan

Lived Hideaki Nakamura of the Black Lotus Clan

A group of assassins that live by the sword

That would destroy a whole village if given the word

Hideaki was ruthless and cared for no one

Which earned him the title of number one shogun

But even the heartless can find themselves a heart

For love is a concept as complicated as art

He fell for Keiko Okowa of the Bamboo clan

Despite being cursed if he were to take her hand

He could not help himself from the sight when they met

Watching the sun gleam from her body while wet

As she bathed in a river by a small water fall

He declared that her beauty had far surpassed all

As he approached he saw something in the corner of his eye

It was her personal body guards; master samurai

Standing a few yards away looking quite apathetic

Hideaki could not help but find them pathetic

He grabbed two rocks and threw them with ease

They shot through the samurai quietly and then through some trees

Then went on his way arrogantly to claim his prize

But when he reached her he was in for a surprise

She stood in her underwear with a sword in his face

Disregarding it he looked down and complimented her taste

Keiko could not help but fall for his boyish charm

So she moved the sword from his face and rested it on her arm

Confidently he told her she was the prettiest girl in the whole world

And asked her if she would be his girl

She said, "To marry me you'd have to be a fool.

If you marry me you will be cursed too."

Quickly he told her if they got married he could lift the spell

Because he knew the greatest magician quite well

A smile grew on her face and she agreed to wed

If only Hideaki knew that he was getting in way over his head.

They both planned the wedding to take place in fall

But when word reached the Bamboo Clan they swore to kill them all

The Bamboo clan planned to kill the Black Lotus at the wedding

For their sinister leader could think of no better setting

And make Hideaki an example for all to see

By placing his head atop a bamboo tree

So he prepared his warriors for the fight of the century

For this time he would show the Black Lotus no mercy

Hideaki had sent word to his friend the magician

To work his expertise to solve his bride's situation

But when he examined her aura he had terrible news

Which angered Hideaki who had such a short fuse

The magician tried and tried again to find a solution

But time and time again he found no resolution

The magician told them it was no ordinary spell

Whomever casted it knew their magic quite well

The best he could do was minimize its potency

So it will only affect them and not touch their legacy

He casted his spell and went on his way

Saying that he will return another day

But before he was gone he left them a warning

That something quite dangerous was coming

Unfortunately Hideaki was not listening

Because he was lost in Keiko's eyes that were glistening

With happiness that she felt for their unborn child

Knowing the curse would not affect them made it all worthwhile

They both held each other and had their lips locked together

As lotus blossoms twirled around them, their spirits synched with nature

The fallen pedals covered them like a protective cocoon

While the both made love under the light of the moon

From far in the distance a leader watches in disgust

As Keiko was once someone he held significant lust

He waived off his spies and headed back to base

Somehow feeling that his clan had been disgraced

The entire ride home he rode with a tightly clinched fist

In his mind he felt sorry that it had to end like this

He knew that he would soon get his revenge

And he would show no mercy to his childhood friend

That night he practiced his combat through deep meditation
Mastering his technique and honing his concentration
Imagining how his fight with Hideaki would transpire
He imagined them both in the middle of a village on fire
Clashing swords with unspeakable power
The pleasure he would have as Keiko watched Hideaki's final hour
Watching over and over the moment of Hideaki's death
Then with a relieving sigh, he took a deep breath
An evil smile appeared on his face no normal person could handle
And he leaned down before him and blew out the candle
Many seasons had passed and it was now fall
Hideaki invited everyone to the wedding, one and all
There were singers, dancers, musicians, women, and spirits
The music was so loud all of Japan could hear it.
Keiko and Hideaki both wore black
Except for their clan's insignia on their backs
After all it made for great advertisement
What kind of gang would they be if they didn't represent
They partied all afternoon straight into sunset
Eating and drinking amounts that everyone would soon regret
Until it was finally time for the ceremony
The moment Keiko and Hideaki awaited with much anxiety
Everyone silenced each other and even the cows
So they could all hear them recite their vows

But before the "I do" something went terribly awry

As blood splattered from the monk's right eye

They both saw the arrow sticking out of his head

A good indication that the monk was probably dead

Hideaki immediately called for his men to protect his bride

And that if they failed he would have all their hides

They all came together forming a human shield

Standing ready for battle ready to kill without yield

But the moment that followed took them all by surprise

As thousands of fiery arrows reddened the dark blue sky

All stood quietly and made not a sound

Even when all flaming arrows plummeted towards the ground

Hideaki swung with his sword creating massive winds

Diverting the arrows away from his bride and friends

Because he was angry his accuracy was flawed

A few burning arrows had struck someone's wall

In a matter of moments the whole house was on fire

As if the situation at hand was not already dire

Burning embers caught in the wind spreading throughout the village

Then enters the Bamboo Clan to rape and to pillage

Both clans charge at each other with hearts full of rage

Thirsting for blood as neither had seen any in days

As Hideaki watched the battle he heard a voice from behind

A familiar voice he had kept in the back of his mind

It was a voice he had not heard in years

The sound of it almost brought Hideaki to tears

Hideaki asked, "Why have you ruined my wedding day?"

"I have come, little brother, to make you pay

Keiko was mine and you stole her from me

And for that, little brother, I will show you no mercy."

"Dammit Hiroki I should have finished you off when I had the chance

Before you became the leader of that damn Bamboo clan."

They stared at each other then pulled out their swords

Because they both knew this bitter rivalry went deeper than words.

With each passing moment their hatred grew within

They both took their stance for the madness about to begin

Meanwhile behind a human shield did Keiko see

Her husband to be squaring off with her old lover Hiroki

She could do nothing but watch in fear

Hoping that Hideaki's death was not near

Smoke and flames quickly rise to the sky

And both master warriors disappeared in the blink of an eye

Running towards each other at the speed of light

Their swords came together displaying incredible might

Cracks and craters were forming under their feet

Opposing auras clash causing heavy static electricity

Despite Hideaki's efforts Hiroki was standing strong

Something about him seemed terribly wrong.

Hiroki held off Hideaki without breaking a sweat

A factor that Hideaki took as an alarming threat

The sparks from their swords flew as they grew near

And during the struggle Hiroki whispered something in his ear

Putting scenarios in his head that he could not take lightly

That consequently caused Hideaki to let his guard down slightly

Which was just enough for Hiroki to make his next move

And use a technique only the Bamboo Clan could use

He channeled the power of the Earth deities

To summon forth a small patch of bamboo trees

That grew under his foes feet at an astonishing pace

Straight up in the air towards the black voids of space

However Hideaki managed to catch a lucky break

By diving out of the way leaving him almost unscathed

Suffering only a small cut to his right eye

He got up, cut down the trees, and got back in the fight

It was time he showed his brother his own special technique

One that would dramatically increase his stamina and physique

Placing a posed hand to his chest he started to chant

While Hiroki watched curiously from a defensive stance

Hideaki's body blazed red and his eyes glowed blue

Hiroki stared anxiously to learn what he was trying to do

Finally the moment came when his body grew large

His kimono shred to pieces when he flexed both his arms

With his newly gained mass he walked towards his enemy

But Hiroki stood there and looked at him calmly

Using his muscular arms he lifted a massive piece of land

And threw it at Hiroki with a single hand

It flew towards his brother with the speed of a bullet

However his sturdy katana was able to cut through it

Hideaki watched the mass of land with awe as it parted

Feeling pissed off when Hiroki asked, "Ready to get started?"

Screaming and bloodshed continued nearby

As the clans took heavy casualties on both sides

Keiko was no longer shielded by Hideaki's best men

And in their absence was forced to pick up her sword once again

She slashed her way through those that were once her friends

The meaning of this battle was something she could not comprehend

All she knew was that it had to end once and for all

Even if t meant that her old lover Hiroki must fall

So she battled her way to where Hideaki and Hiroki fought

To help kill a man that she undoubtedly brought

But as she came nearer her heart filled with guilt

For destroying two clans that each man had built

She could not stop now and had to move on

Despite being exhausted for it was almost dawn

They were so close she could hear the swords clash

And from the sound of the fight they were evenly matched

Faster and faster the clashing became

The thought of the fight drove her completely insane

Until all went completely silent

When just an instant ago the fight sounded quite violent

Keiko could only suspect that someone had won

And questioned the fate of the number one shogun

Until the moment had come when she could finally see
Which brought her lamentably down to her knees
Thunder and lightning sound and flash overhead
Rain rinsing away ashes and blood from the dead
Overtaken with grief from the overwhelming view
With Hideaki's wakizashi Keiko committed seppuku
Keiko's body fell amongst the two dead brothers
That, while in battle, had stabbed one another
Now huddled together, an arm around each other's throat
The blade's tip through their backs evidently show
So it appeared that the curse had conquered them all
And from that day forward it was passed into law
That samurai would no longer be allowed to walk the Earth
For they were more trouble than they were actually worth
The government was ordered to look all around
But the bodies of these warriors were never found
Thanks to the magician and the wave of his hand
That turned each of their bodies into black sand
Which he then buried while laughing and singing
As he believed this tragedy could start a new beginning

ABOUT THE AUTHOR

Michael Richardson Jr. was born in 1986 in Bellflower, California to Byllie Karen and Michael Richardson. He has two younger brothers named Jordon and Aaron. Michael currently resides in Ontario, California where he graduated from Ontario High School. He is now a student at Cal State San Bernardino where he plans to achieve his master's degree in psychology. When he is not studying or in class Michael likes to jot down interesting ideas about the darker side of life and use them for poems or short stories.

NOTE FROM THE AUTHOR

They say it takes a village to raise a child. I believe the same concept can be applied in creating great poets. With Juvenile and Nonsensical being my first book, it would be safe to say that I am still a child in the grand scheme of poetry and writing in general. There is still much to learn as poetry is such a complex art form. With this thought in mind I would like to inform everyone that their feedback is always welcomed and encouraged.

"Alone we can do so little; together we can do so much."

Helen Keller

Please visit my blog at http://juvenileandnonsensical.blogspot.com/

For news on upcoming projects

Or e-mail me at

Juvenile_Nonsensical@yahoo.com